D0883710

Twenty
Names In
ART

Alan Blackwood

Illustrated by Edward Mortelmans

MARSHALL CAVENDISH
New York, London, Toronto

Editor: Rosemary Ashley
Consultant Editor: Maggi McCormick

Reference Edition published 1988

© Marshall Cavendish Limited 1988
© Wayland (Publishers) Limited 1988

Published by Marshall Cavendish Corporation
147 West Merrick Road
Freeport
Long Island
N.Y. 11520

Library of Congress Cataloging in Publication Data

Blackwood, Alan, 1932-
    Twenty names in art / Alan Blackwood
        p. cm. — (Twenty names)
    Bibliography: p.
    Includes index.
    Summary: A collection of brief biographies of twenty famous artists
    ISBN 0-86307-972-5 : $12.95
    1. Artists-Biography-Juvenile literature. [1. Artists.]
I. Title. II. Title: 20 names in art. III. Series.
N42, B54 1988
709' .2'2-dc19
[B]   88-20991
[920]   CIP
                                AC

Printed in Italy by G. Canale & C. S.p.A. - Turin.

Contents

The world of art   4
1   Hieronymous Bosch   6
2   Leonardo da Vinci   8
3   Albrecht Dürer   10
4   Michelangelo   12
5   El Greco   14
6   Rembrandt   16
7   William Hogarth   18
8   Hokusai   20
9   J. M. W. Turner   22
10 Claude Monet   24
11 Berthe Morisot   26
12 Vincent Van Gogh   28
13 Henry Ossawa Tanner   30
14 Rabindranath Tagore   32
15 Käthe Kollwitz   34
16 Pablo Picasso   36
17 Henry Moore   38
18 Salvadore Dali   40
19 Sydney Nolan   42
20 Andy Warhol   44
Glossary   46
Further Reading   46
Index   47

The world of art

Thirty thousand years ago, people painted images of wild animals on the walls of caves. They believed painting was a kind of magic that would help them in their hunt for real animals to use for food and clothing. The ancient Egyptians believed that painting pictures of gods and goddesses on the walls and ceilings of burial chambers would aid the dead on their way to the afterlife. Ancient Greek and Roman sculptors carved figures of gods and heroes on their temples and monuments because they believed these figures encouraged people to have faith in their religion and pride in their history.

We take up the story in sixteenth-century Europe, when artists were working in great churches and cathedrals, or in the palaces of kings, queens, and popes. In the following pages, we meet Leonardo da Vinci, Michelangelo, El Greco, Rembrandt, Monet, Van Gogh, Picasso,

4

and many others; artists of genius, whose master-pieces are known and loved by people everywhere. We meet, too, such talented painters as Berthe Morisot and Henry Ossawa Tanner, to remind us how many gifted women and black artists there have been, and how hard they have had to fight to gain recognition. There is also Rabindranath Tagore, the great Indian poet and philosopher, who turned to painting to express some of his deepest thoughts and feelings.

The paintings, drawings, and sculptures of these and other great artists present us with an amazing variety of styles and ideas, from five hundred years ago to the present day. So, we learn about chiaroscuro and fresco painting, impressionist, cubist, surrealist, abstract, and pop art. Artists must be craftsmen and technicians, as well as creative men and women. Through their work, we learn, too, about such techniques as woodcuts, engraving, etching, metal casting, silk-screen printing, and the use of oils and watercolors.

1
Hieronymous Bosch

Five hundred years ago, most people believed that hell was an actual place, full of fire and smoke. It was the place of punishment for those who had led wicked, sinful lives. People also believed there were demons and other evil beings, watching them and tempting them to sin, so that their souls would end up in hell.

As a warning to people to lead virtuous lives, the Church paid artists to paint, or carve in stone, pictures of hell and of demons. Hieronymous Bosch was one of these artists. His real name was Jeroen Anthoiszoon, but he adopted the surname of Bosch from the town where he was born, Hertogenbosch, now in Holland. To the people of the town, he appeared a quiet, peaceful man; but his imagination was peopled with demons and monsters driving human beings to hell and damnation.

1450 born in Hertogenbosch, Holland
1480 marries and inherits property, providing him with a comfortable income for life
1510 paints his famous triptych, *The Garden of Earthly Delights*
1516 dies in his hometown

Right *Bosch found inspiration to paint some of his strange, fantastic pictures in the twisted shapes and patterns of plants.*

Bosch's paintings show us that strange world. They are nightmarish visions of landscapes filled with strange people and monsters, painted in meticulous detail and in bright, clear colors, as though he really could see them. The most famous of his works is a triptych (a painting in three sections that can be opened like a book) called *The Garden of Earthly Delights*. The center panel is entitled *The Seven Deadly Sins*.

In the sixteenth century, The Netherlands (now Holland) was ruled by Spain. The Spanish King, Philip II, was fascinated by Bosch's painting and had them hung in his palaces. Today, some of the best of Bosch's works are in the Prado Museum in Madrid. His paintings are even more popular in this century. Many people are fascinated by them and consider Bosch to have been many centuries ahead of his time in revealing the half-hidden fantasies and fears that exist in the human mind.

The Parable of the Sower *shows clearly how Bosch combined religious subjects with his own fantasies. Notice the strange figure, half-man, half-beast, on the horse.*

2
Leonardo da Vinci

Leonardo da Vinci lived during the period of history called the Renaissance, meaning a rebirth or new quest for knowledge. In addition to painting and sculpture, he studied mathematics, anatomy, botany, zoology, optics, mechanics, and engineering. He examined fossils and wrote about the origins of life. He drew up plans for a city. He is known as the greatest "Renaissance Man," because he was interested in everything.

Leonardo was born in Vinci, in the Tuscany region of Italy (hence his full name). At the age of fifteen, he was apprenticed to the Florentine artist Verrocchio; and, in the studio, he studied the new art of perspective – creating the illusion of distance on a flat surface, based on the principles of geometry. Leonardo believed that light and color were just as important as perspective in creating an impression of distance and depth.

Below *Leonardo was fascinated by everything around him. He painted some of the world's greatest masterpieces, and he noted his scientific observations in thousands of drawings.*

One of Leonardo's patrons was Duke Lodovici Sforza of Milan, and it was in that city that he produced his first masterpiece, *The Last Supper*, painted on a wall of the monastery of Santa Maria delle Grazie. In Florence, he worked for Cesare Borgia – the most notorious member of a powerful Florentine ruling family. There, he produced the world's most famous painting, the *Mona Lisa*, the portrait of a merchant's wife.

All the time, Leonardo was looking at the world of people and of nature with more curiosity and intensity than anyone had done before him, and recording his observations and thoughts in hundreds of marvelous scientific drawings and notes. He even designed a flying machine and an underwater machine, four centuries before the invention of airplanes and submarines.

At the end of his long life, Leonardo was invited to France by King Francis I. Three years later, he died there, after a life of amazing achievement.

The Mona Lisa, *in the Louvre Museum, Paris. The smile on the lady's face introduced a new and more personal style of portrait painting.*

1452	born at Vinci, near Florence, Italy
1483	settles in Milan
1485	paints *The Virgin of the Rocks*
1497	paints mural of *The Last Supper* at monastery of St. Maria delle Grazie, Milan
1502	becomes Cesare Borgia's military adviser in Florence
c1504	paints the *Mona Lisa* portrait
1516	invited to work in France by King Francis I
1519	dies near Amboise, France

3
Albrecht Dürer

Most of the famous artists of the Renaissance were Italians. But Albrecht Dürer was German, the son of a goldsmith. He was born in Nuremberg, a proud and prosperous city which stood at the crossroads of important overland trade routes and was renowned for its crafts and industries.

As a young man, he visited Italy and was very excited by all he saw and learned there. He became one of the most skilled and versatile artists in many of the new styles and techniques of the time – using black and white paints on colored paper, pen and charcoal drawing, and painting watercolor landscapes. He also produced some of the first great self-portraits.

Returning to Germany, Dürer discovered the new art and craft of printing, which excited him most of all. He carved superb woodcuts and

1471 born in Nuremburg, Germany
1490–4 travels to Colmar, Basle, and Strasbourg
1490 visits Venice
1498 produces his famous set of woodcuts on the Apocalypse
1528 dies in Nuremburg

Right *Dürer was a master engraver. Engraving was the newest and most advanced printing technology of his time.*

perfected the even newer art of engraving on a copper plate, as ways of printing illustrations. He combined this work with his religious ideas, inspired by the teaching of the German Reformation leader, Martin Luther. His woodcuts and engravings of Bible scenes, especially the very vivid and dramatic illustrations of the Apocalypse (visions of the end of the world) brought him fame and commissions for more work from some of the greatest rulers of the age. Many of his drawings and studies are now in public art collections in Europe and the United States.

Like Leonardo da Vinci, Dürer also had the inquiring mind of a scientist, and he wrote important essays on the mathematical principles of art and design. By his work and his ceaseless quest for knowledge and new skills, he was a true man of the Renaissance, helping to spread its ideas right across Europe.

This famous study of a pair of hands shows clearly Dürer's marvelous eye for detail and his control of line and shade.

4
Michelangelo

Michelangelo Buonarotti came from the same region of Italy as Leonardo da Vinci, and he was the other giant among all the great figures of the Renaissance. The violent events surrounding his life added a special quality of drama and tension to his work.

Michelangelo was a student in Florence when his patron, Lorenzo de Medici, was expelled from the city by Savonarola, the reforming monk who was later burned at the stake on the orders of the Pope.

In 1501, Michelangelo produced his great statue of David, which he sculpted from a block of marble that other artists said they couldn't use. Then, the new Pope, Julius II, summoned him to Rome to design and build a massive memorial tomb. No sooner had Michelangelo drawn up his plans, than Julius commanded him instead to begin decorating the Sistine Chapel, in the Vatican, with fresco paintings. During the years 1508

1475 born near Florence, Italy
1501 begins work on the statue of David in Florence
1505 summoned to Rome to design memorial tomb for Pope Julius II
1508–12 begins work on the painting of the Sistine Chapel, Rome
1527 takes part in the defence of Florence against Pope Clement VIII
1537 adds the painting *The Last Judgment* to the altar wall of the Sistine Chapel
1547 appointed chief architect of the new basilica of St. Peter's, Rome
1564 dies in Rome, age 89

to 1512, Michelangelo toiled away, standing or lying awkwardly, covering first the ceiling and later, in 1537, the walls, with such tremendous Bible scenes as *The Creation of Adam* and *The Last Judgment*, proving that he was a great painter as well as a great sculptor.

But wars and feuds interrupted Michelangelo's life again. His great bronze statue of Julius was melted down to make cannon. He helped to defend Florence against yet another Pope. When Florence was captured, Michelangelo hid in fear from the Pope's soldiers.

Finally, he was forgiven and put in charge of the construction of the new building of St. Peter's Basilica in Rome. He designed the colossal dome, 435 ft. high, that was completed after his death.

Throughout his turbulent life, Michelangelo had to leave many projects unfinished. But, by the time of his death at eighty-nine, he had left behind him, in buildings, sculptures, and paintings, some of the world's greatest works of art.

Above *Michelangelo was above all a sculptor. His* Pietà, *the Virgin Mary with the body of Christ, is in St. Peter's, Rome.*

Below *Michelangelo shows his plans for a memorial tomb to Pope Julius II.*

5
El Greco

"El Greco" is Spanish for "The Greek." The artist known as El Greco was actually born on the island of Crete, and his real name was Domenicos Theotocopoulos. He first went to Venice, where he studied with the celebrated Renaissance artist Titian; then, he spent some time in Rome. Finally, in 1577, he moved to Toledo in Spain, where he spent the rest of his life.

Sixteenth-century Spain was experiencing an extremely religious period of its history. Among the Spanish saints and mystics of the time were St. Teresa of Avila, who wrote about her spiritual visions, and St. Ignatius Loyola, who founded the Society of Jesus (the Jesuits). The Inquisition, the organization intended to stamp out heresy – any ideas or beliefs that challenged official Church doctrine – also flourished during the period.

El Greco was deeply influenced by all this

Below *The artist at work in his studio in Toledo.*

intense religious feeling and turmoil around him, and it is reflected in his paintings. He used only five basic colors on his palette, as though he were imposing upon himself an artistic and spiritual discipline; but he combined these colors in a way that made his paintings glow with a strange, whitish light. And, he often portrayed people in an oddly distorted way, making them appear as part of some mystical vision or trance. One of his most famous paintings is the altarpiece for Toledo Cathedral. Another is *The Burial of Count Orgaz*, which is in the church of St. Tome in Toledo. The Count, one of his patrons, is shown ascending to heaven. His *View of Toledo* is not a religious picture, but he used the same techniques to make the city appear to rise into the sky above the rugged Spanish landscape.

El Greco belonged to the Baroque period of art, when artists and architects built and painted on a grand and dramatic scale, but nobody before or since has painted pictures as he did.

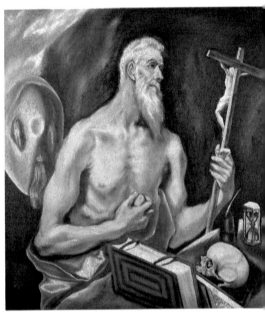

This study of St. Jerome, in the Prado Museum, Madrid, is a fine example of El Greco's style, seeming to glow with a strange, mystical light.

1541	born on the island of Crete
1560	travels to Italy, works in Venice and Rome
1577	travels to Spain and settles in Toledo
1579	paints altarpieces *The Trinity* and *Assumption* for the Cathedral of San Domingo
1586	paints *The Burial of Count Orgaz*
1614	dies in Toledo

6
Rembrandt

The Dutch painter Rembrandt van Rijn was born in Leyden, the son of a miller, at the time when Holland became an independent nation. He had a brilliant start to his career. As a young man, he was in great demand as a portrait painter, he was happily married (his wife Saskia was also rich), and he enjoyed all the good things of life.

Quite suddenly, all that changed. Saskia died, and Rembrandt began to work in a way that was not appreciated by most of his friends and clients. The painting that best marked this change of style is *The Night Watch*, now in the Rijksmuseum, Amsterdam. The painting, in fact, is meant to be a daytime scene. It depicts a group of militiamen, but Rembrandt was becoming so interested in painting contrasts of light and shade that several members of the group are in shadow. This did not please the people concerned, who complained that they couldn't be seen!

1606 born in Leiden, Holland
1632 paints *The Anatomy Lesson*
1634 marries Saskia van Vylenborch,
paints *Portrait of himself with Saskia*
1642 Saskia dies; paints his most famous picture, *The Night Watch*
1662 paints the *Staal Meesters*
1669 dies in Amsterdam

Right *The artist sketching a winter scene in Holland. Rembrandt and other Dutch artists were among the first great landscape painters.*

The style, the effect of light and shade that Rembrandt concentrated on afterward, is called "chiaroscuro." This style had already been used very dramatically by the Italian Baroque painter, Caravaggio. Rembrandt's work in chiaroscuro lost him his fashionable clientele and his main source of income. In 1656, his house and possessions were auctioned to pay his debts. This change in his circumstances did not deter him; and his paintings, often of subjects taken from the Bible or ancient history, became ever more rich and splendid, as though illuminated from within by a golden glow of light. He achieved a similar effect of light and shade in hundreds of black and white etchings.

Throughout his life, Rembrandt also painted many self-portraits. They show him changing from the carefree artist of his youth to a sad and lonely old man. These wonderful paintings are the most moving series of self-portraits in the whole history of art.

Rembrandt's portrait of his son, Titus. Note how the lighted face stands out against the surrounding shadow.

7
William Hogarth

The English painter and engraver William Hogarth lived in London in the eighteenth century, when it had become the capital of a mighty empire, a great seaport, and the largest city in the world. It was also the place where some of the first newspapers were published, and ideas and information began to spread among all classes of people. Hogarth used his art almost like a form of journalism, to report upon aspects of the life and times of his day.

Hogarth presented, rather like scenes from a play, a series of paintings showing the downfall of frivolous and stupid people in a rich and corrupt society. He had an unerring eye for human failings. His first series, *The Harlot's Progress*, depicted the downfall of a country girl at the hands of wicked Londoners. Other series were *The Rake's Progress* and *Marriage à la mode*.

Right *Hogarth used his art to report on the frailties of his fellow humans. Here, he is observing drunkenness in a London street.*

1697 born in London
1729 marries the daughter of rich painter Sir James Thornhill
1732–3 produces his series of paintings, *The Harlot's Progress* and *The Rakes Progress*
1742 paints *Marriage à la mode*
1754 paints *The Election*
1764 dies in London

In his many black and white engravings, he portrayed some of the miseries of life for London's poor people. *Gin Lane* is a shocking study of public drunkenness. Other engravings are not so grim. They show people enjoying themselves at the theater, gambling, and watching sporting events, or taking part in some of the first parliamentary elections, which were riotous affairs in those days. Nobody before Hogarth had depicted everyday life with such accuracy or with such a sharp eye for caricature, and today his pictures are a valuable historical record, giving us an insight into the lives of the ordinary people of the time.

Hogarth's attitude to his art was new in another way. He operated for much of his life like a businessman, selling printed copies of his engravings at a price ordinary people could afford. In this way, he also pioneered the idea of commerical and popular art.

Hogarth depicted the evils of drink in this famous engraving – entitled Gin Lane.

8
Hokusai

For thousands of years, there was almost no contact between Western, or European, civilization and the cultures of the Far East, notably those of China and Japan. Marco Polo's epic thirteenth-century journey to China and back, and his account of the wondrous things he had seen, first opened the door to East–West relations. From then on, more and more European merchants and missionaries went to China, returning home with examples of Chinese porcelain and painting, which inspired new fashions in Western art and design. Japan was more inaccessible than China, but eventually, in the sixteenth century, Europeans reached that country, too. Japanese artists were interested to see prints and paintings from Europe, and the work of Japanese artists, in turn, was much appreciated by people in Europe and America.

1760 born in Edo (Tokyo), Japan

1755 apprenticed to woodblock engraver and later to the artist Katsukawa

1780 produces first *Ukiyo-ye* paintings

1834–5 produces celebrated series of prints, *Thirty-six Views of Mount Fuji* including the celebrated "Breaking Wave of Kanagawa"

1849 dies in Edo

One of these artists was Kasushika Hokusai. His specialty was producing colored prints from woodblocks, using a separate block of wood for each color. These belonged to a tradition of Japanese art called *Ukiyo-ye*, or "Floating World" – images of little groups of people going about their work or play, or scenes from nature. Hokusai learned something about the use of color from studying European prints; but his own work retained all the delicacy, fine craftsmanship, and detail of so much oriental art. He made hundreds of "Floating World" prints of such scenes as Mount Fujiyama, the beautiful volcano near Tokyo, and one very famous image of a great ocean wave.

Copies of Hokusai's prints found their way to Paris, where their delicate line and color was greatly admired. His style was copied by such masters as Edouard Manet, Henri Toulouse-Lautrec, and Edgar Degas, and so has influenced the course of Western art.

One of Hokusai's thirty-six exquisite prints of Mount Fuji. The outline of the mountain rises up in the background.

Below *The artist working in the peace and beauty of the Japanese countryside.*

9
J. M. W. Turner

Joseph Mallord William Turner, one of the great masters of landscape painting, was born in London in 1775. He began painting seriously at the early age of fourteen, when there was already a strong tradition of landscape painting, especially among Dutch and English artists. Turner followed in this tradition, painting many scenes of the English countryside. He also traveled abroad to paint in France, Germany, Switzerland, and Italy. He produced thousands of paintings, from huge canvases in oil to small, delicate watercolors, as though he could hardly capture fast enough all the sights and impressions that excited him.

Turner's early paintings, already masterly and beautiful, are comparatively straightforward – they show the detailed scenes that his viewers expected. But, as his style and technique developed, he began to concentrate on certain features, such as sunlight reflected on water as

Below *Turner's early paintings were exhibited at the Royal Academy and were much admired by fashionable society. But, his later work mystified most people.*

he had seen it in Venice, or the sun seen at dawn or sunset through a haze of clouds, or on the patterns of light created by wind-driven rain or swirling snow. Turner was also fascinated by the smoke and fire of the new industrial age of the late eighteenth and early nineteenth centuries, and by steamships and trains. Two of his most famous paintings, *The Fighting Temeraire* and *Rain, Wind and Speed,* are inspired by these subjects. His last paintings are almost totally abstract studies of sun and sky, rain and water. Turner lived before the French Impressionists, whose work we shall soon be discussing, but he anticipated their ideas and techniques by forty years.

Many people now regard this revolutionary painter, who had virtually no education and never learned to read or write, as the greatest of all British artists. In 1986, a special new wing was added to the Tate Gallery in London to house a large part of Turner's huge collection of works.

An ocean scene near the Bay of Naples. It is a fine example of Turner's wonderful treatment of water, sunlight, and cloud.

1775	born in London
1790	first watercolors exhibited at the Royal Academy
1797	exhibits oil paintings at Royal Academy
1802	elected member of the Royal Academy; first journey abroad
1803	paints *Calais Pier*
1817–19	visits Germany and Italy
1835–40	visits Venice, produces "Venetian watercolors"
1838	paints *The Fighting Temeraire*
1851	dies in London

10
Claude Monet

One of today's best-loved "schools," or groups of artists, is the Impressionists. The man who gave their work this name was the French artist, Claude Monet, when he painted a picture entitled *Impression – Sunrise*. Monet grew up near the River Seine in France, and he loved to paint the reflections in the river. He produced natural light effects by using swifts dabs of color to create an impression of his subject.

The term "Impressionist" was first used in a mocking way, by people who didn't understand such pictures. It is, however, a good name for the new style of painting that Monet and his colleagues were creating. The invention of photography earlier in the nineteenth century had completely changed the role of artists. They were no longer required to present life-like portraits or careful records of places or events. The camera could do that. Instead, they began to explore new

Below *Monet's fascination with water prompted him to paint many of his pictures in a boat – his "floating studio."*

techniques, new ways of suggesting the special atmosphere of a scene – things that, in those days, the camera could not do.

On a visit to London, Monet saw some of Turner's paintings, and began to develop further that artist's treatment of sky, clouds, water, and sun. Monet aimed to capture the passing "impression" of shimmering sunlight on sea, or the steam and smoke of a railway station. He painted trees that seem almost to rustle in the wind, and water that seems to ripple as you look at it. And to study the effects of light, he painted the same building, Rouen Cathedral, as it appeared to him at different times of day, from dawn till dusk.

As he grew older, Monet began to go blind, but he could still see enough to paint the water lilies in his garden pond, colors and shapes seeming to dissolve into each other. This garden, near the River Seine in France, has been kept as the painter knew it, and is visited every year by thousands of lovers of his magical art.

This shimmering study of poplar trees beside a river is in the Scottish National Gallery in Edinburgh. It is a masterpiece of impressionist art.

1840 born in Paris
1870 visits London, studies paintings of Turner and Constable
1874 first Impressionist Exhibition in Paris, named after his own painting, *Impression – Sunrise*
1892–5 produces famous series of paintings of Rouen cathedral
1899–1904 paints *Thames* series
1916 paints *Waterlilies* at his home in Giverny, near Paris
1926 dies at Giverny

11
Berthe Morisot

There have been many famous women authors and poets. There have also been many talented women artists, but, only in fairly recent times, have they begun to make a name for themselves.

One of the first to do so was the French painter Berthe Morisot. She lived in the last century, when nearly everyone believed that "a woman's place is in the home." So, Berthe Morisot had to combat all kinds of prejudice when she decided to become a serious painter. There were, however, some factors strongly in her favor. Her great grandfather was Jean Fragonard, one of the most celebrated artists of the eighteenth-century "Rococo" period of art; and her mother encouraged her to paint, despite the disapproval of other members of the family. Also, one of her teachers was the great nineteenth-century French landscape artist, Jean-Baptiste Corot.

Below *Like the other impressionist painters, Berthe Morisot did much of her work in the open air.*

The event that largely shaped Morisot's painting career was her marriage to Eugene Manet, brother of the Impressionist painter Edouard Manet. This brought her into close contact with some of the other Impressionists, including Auguste Renoir. She began to paint along the same impressionist lines, although in her own highly individual way. Her strong use of color influenced Manet himself (who, in turn, painted several portraits of her). In her paintings, many of women and children, Morisot captured the beauty of the "fleeting moment."

As an Impressionist painter and a woman, she had to cope with even more criticism and abuse than her male colleagues had received when their work was first shown in public. By her pioneering example, Berthe Morisot helped to achieve recognition for women artists who, over the centuries and even in our own times, still do not always receive the acknowledgement that they should.

This study of a wheat field hangs in the Orsay Museum in Paris.

1841	born in Bourges, France
1862	studies with the landscape artist Jean-Baptiste Corot
1873	paints *The Artist's Sister* and *The Cradle*
1874	marries Eugene Manet and contributes paintings for the First Impressionist Exhibition in Paris
1895	dies in Paris

12

Vincent Van Gogh

"I want to say something comforting," wrote the Dutchman Vincent Van Gogh, in one of his many letters to his brother, Theo. What he also wanted to find was happiness. But he never did.

Before he turned to art, Van Gogh was a missionary priest, working among the poor people of industrial Belgium and northern France. He shared their poverty and hardships, and his first drawings and paintings express his love and sympathy for them. In 1885, he painted *The Potato Eaters*, a haunting scene of peasant poverty. Then, he went to Paris, where Theo was an art dealer. There, he met some of the Impressionists and began copying their style.

The event that really changed Van Gogh's life was his move to Arles, in the south of France. The bright, clear light of Provence stirred him to a frenzy of excitement. He began applying paints

1853 born in Groot-Zundert, Holland
1868 works with art dealer in The Hague, London, and Paris
1880 begins drawing and painting among poor people of French and Belgian coalfields
1886 moves to Paris and studies Impressionist paintings
1888 lives in Arles, in southern France, paints numerous landscapes, portraits, and *Sunflowers*
1889 has fit of madness and cuts off his ear, enters asylum in St. Remy
1890 returns to Paris, commits suicide

to his canvases with thick heavy strokes, twists, and swirls of the brush. He worked at great speed, painting the fields and canals around Arles and portraits of the local people. For his own room, he painted pictures of sunflowers. He went much further than the Impressionists, using his art to express his own moods and passions.

Van Gogh was still not happy. He quarreled with the artist, Paul Gauguin, who came to stay with him, and in a fit of madness cut off one of his own ears. He recovered in a hospital near the town of St. Remy de Provence, and painted more landscapes that danced with life and color. He returned north to live with a doctor outside Paris. One day, while out painting in the fields, he committed suicide by shooting himself.

Van Gogh never lived to see the tremendous influence his vivid use of color had on other artists; nor how much pleasure his pictures have brought to millions of people.

Above *The artist painted this picture of his own humble bedroom in Arles.*

Below *Van Gogh working in the countryside near Arles. Behind him is a field of his beloved sunflowers.*

13
Henry Ossawa Tanner

Henry Ossawa Tanner was born in Pittsburgh, Pennsylvania, at a time when many of his fellow black Americans were still slaves. His father was a bishop in the African Episcopal Church. At the age of thirteen, Henry decided he would become "a great painter." As a student, he endured poverty and ill health, and it took tremendous courage for him to become an artist. He suffered many hardships, working all day in manual jobs to save just enough money to study art in the little spare time that he had.

In 1890, after many disappointments, Tanner left the United States and went to live in Paris, at that time a world center for art and artists. He was still very short of money, but he continued to struggle, determined to prove himself as a great painter. At one time, he nearly starved and

became very ill. At last, he realized the dream of every struggling artist in Paris – one of his pictures was accepted by the Salon, an annual display of work by new artists.

Soon, everybody was talking about his paintings of Bible scenes, such as *Daniel in the Lion's Den* and *Moses and the Burning Bush*. At the same time, his *Raising of Lazarus* was being exhibited back in the United States. Tanner learned a great deal about the techniques of painting color and light from the Impressionists; but he filled his pictures also with his own very personal religious feelings. His work was so much admired in France that he was made a member of the French Legion of Honor – a unique distinction. He found in France a freedom from racial prejudice that did not exist in his own country. But he was also honored in the United States, and art galleries across America were proud to show his work.

1859	born in Pittsburgh studies at the Academy of Fine Arts, Philadelphia
1890	travels to Paris
1900	wins award at the Paris Universal Exhibition
c1901	travels to Palestine
1928	created Chevalier of the French Legion of Honor
1937	dies in Paris

The artist endured hardship and illness in his cold Paris studio before his work was finally recognized.

14
Rabindranath Tagore

We have read, on page 20, of the Japanese painter Kasushika Hokusai, and how he had a strong influence on the work of artists in Europe. Rabindranath Tagore found an even more thorough way to bring together the ancient wisdom of India and Western culture.

Tagore lived during the time of the British Empire; but, like all wise Indians, including his friend Mahatma Gandhi, he knew that the Raj was only a passing episode in the long passage of history. Far more important for him was to speak to as many people as possible around the world. He traveled in Europe, America, and the Far East, lecturing on Indian philosophy and religion, hoping to reconcile Eastern and Western thought. He wrote novels, essays, and poetry, originally in his native tongue of Bengali, but soon translated into English and other languages.

Below *Tagore among his own people, in the Bengali countryside of northeast India.*

In 1913, their truth and beauty earned for him the Nobel Prize for Literature, the highest of all international honors. He also composed music and songs.

Tagore turned to painting last of all, but explained what a dramatic effect art had upon him. "When I started painting," he wrote, "I noticed a great change in my life. I started seeing in trees, branches, and leaves, images of strange creatures." Most of his drawings and paintings are executed with ink or colored crayon on paper. Hardly any of them have a title. They are the "strange creatures" he spoke of, sometimes calm and lovely, sometimes rather menacing faces and figures. There are some landscapes, too; their overall tone or mood is dark and somber.

Tagore's paintings stand halfway between the vision of an Indian mystic and the style of a Western artist, and they are a very valuable link between East and West.

One of Tagore's portraits of an unknown Indian woman.

1861 born in Calcutta, India
1879 visits England and studies at London University
1901 founds school in Bengal for reconciliation of Eastern and Western thought
1913 awarded Nobel Prize for Literature
1915 awarded knighthood, begins long friendship with Gandhi
1928 begins his painting career
1930 first exhibition of drawings and paintings in England and US
1941 dies at his home near Calcutta

15
Käthe Kollwitz

During this century, many artists have been affected by the horrors and miseries of two world wars. One such was Käthe Kollwitz, who was born in Königsberg in East Prussia. She was introduced to the techniques of etching and printing at the age of thirteen and was much impressed by the work of William Hogarth (see page 18). In 1891, she married a doctor, and they settled in a poor district of Berlin.

She soon began producing etchings, woodcuts, and lithographic prints. From the beginning, Kollwitz's work reflected her feelings of protest against the despair of the people around her. Inspired by a play about the desperate plight and revolt of weavers in the industrial region of Silesia, she produced a powerful series of prints, *The Weavers*, which caused a sensation when it was first shown at the Berlin Arts Exhibition in 1898.

1867 born in Konigsberg, then in East Prussia
1891 marries and moves to Berlin
1893–7 *The Weavers* – series of prints
1903–8 *Peasants War* – series of prints
1914 outbreak of First World War – death of son Peter at the front
1922–28 *War* cycle of prints
1933 rise of Hitler – expelled from Berlin Academy
1934–5 eight lithographs on subject of *Death*
1924–32 produces bronze *Pieta*, in Flanders
1945 dies in Germany

Right *Käthe Kollwitz in her Berlin studio, working on one of her powerful pieces of sculpture.*

Kollwitz was deeply affected by the death of her younger son at the front in the World War I (1914–18). During the following years, she began work on a sculptured memorial, finally producing one of her finest works – life-sized figures of mourning parents.

As long as she lived, she never gave up hope. She believed that suffering and persecution could be turned into something beautiful, and her drawings, engravings, and etchings seem to cry out against the unhappiness and injustice she saw around her.

When Hitler and the Nazis came to power in 1933, Kollwitz was expelled from the Berlin Academy of Art and her work banned. She died in 1945, having seen her country reduced to ruin in the Second World War.

Kathe Kollwitz, like many other artists, writers, and composers, demonstrated that deeply-felt political and moral beliefs can also inspire great art.

This study of children begging for food expresses the artist's deep sympathy for the poor.

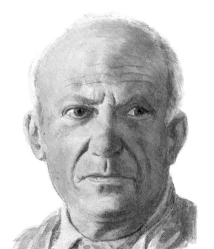

16
Pablo Picasso

Pablo Picasso was born in Spain, but he spent most of his life in France, where he led the way in almost every important development in modern art.

He began painting in a "naturalistic" style, creating life-like portraits of people: his "blue" and "pink" periods, so-called because he worked mainly in those two colors. Then, with the French artist Georges Braque, he pioneered "cubist" art, a revolutionary new way of looking at objects, as though they were composed of geometrical forms such as cubes, triangles, and circles. Sometimes, Picasso and other Cubists pasted such shapes and forms onto a board, producing patterns called collages.

Picasso's next step was to change geometrical shapes into patterns and add stronger colors to them, so creating "abstract" art – that is, abstracting or selecting whatever features he wanted from any scene or object. He was also fascinated by

1881 born in Malaga, Spain
1897 first exhibition of paintings in Madrid
1901 settles in France
1904–6 paintings of "Blue" and "Pink" periods
1907 paints *Demoiselles d'Avignon*, meets Georges Braque and with him evolves the Cubist style
1907–14 paintings of the Cubist period
1937 paints *Guernica* as protest against Spanish Civil War
1973 dies at his home in southern France

the "primitive" art of other civilizations, such as African tribal societies, and began to use their images in his work.

Picasso was often so far ahead of his time that many people did not understand what he was doing. But, a few recognized his brilliance, and he sometimes worked with architects on the decoration of new buildings, as Renaissance and Baroque artists had done in previous centuries.

Picasso held strong opinions about politics, too. He opposed the Fascists in the Spanish Civil War (1936–9); and, when Fascist aircraft bombed Guernica in northern Spain, he produced his most famous painting, *Guernica* (now in the Museum of Modern Art, New York), as a memorial to the people who were killed in the raid.

Picasso could produce humorous as well as serious art; and he went on amazing everybody with his new ideas, in painting, sculpture, engraving, and ceramics, almost up to the day he died at the age of ninety-two. By then, he was hailed as the greatest artist of modern times.

Above Sleeping Girl, *an example of the artist's semi-abstract style.*

Below *Picasso working on one of his ceramic figures. Some of these figures convey his great sense of fun.*

17
Henry Moore

Henry Moore was born in Yorkshire, England, the son of a coal miner. He worked in the same tough way as a miner, hewing with hammer and chisel in stone or wood. He loved the massive stonework of ancient Egypt and of the Mayan civilization of old Mexico, which inspired him to work on a big scale. He was always fascinated by the natural shape and form of rocks, stones, and caves, fashioned over millions of years by the action of wind, rain, ice, and running water. And he believed that the space created within or around a piece of sculpture is as important as the shape of the sculpture itself. Finally, he saw the human body, especially when reclining on its back or side, as another fascinating framework for more shapes and spaces.

Moore's great works of sculpture express all these elements. His works are mostly huge,

Below *The artist wears goggles to protect his eyes from splinters of stone as he works on one of his massive sculptures.*

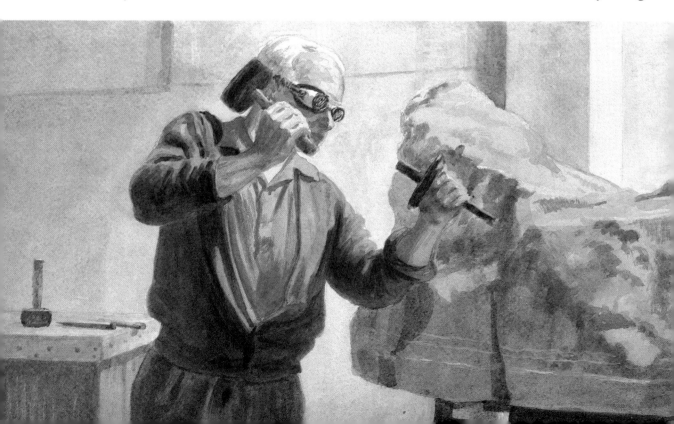

powerful images in stone and wood, or cast in bronze, of large shapes and spaces, sometimes quite life-like, sometimes abstract. They all appear at their best when shown in the open air. Some of his works have been sited on hilltops; some stand proudly outside famous modern buildings, such as the UNESCO Headquarters in Paris and Lincoln Center in New York City. They are all admired as masterpieces of our time.

During the Second World War (1939–45), Moore was an official war artist, and he produced hundreds of drawings and paintings of Londoners sleeping in the underground "tube" stations during the bombing of London. These remarkable studies of the human form, observed under such dramatic circumstances, are another aspect of the work of this great artist, who is recognized as one of the most original and powerful of modern sculptors.

Henry Moore stands next to two of his bronze figures at an exhibition of his work in Florence.

1898 born in Castleford, Yorkshire, England
1919 studies at Leeds College of Art
1921 wins scholarship to Royal College of Art, London
1928 first exhibition of sculpture in London, sculpts *North Wind* for London Underground building
1940–45 official War Artist during Second World War
1944 completes *Madonna and Child* for St. Matthew's Church, Northampton
1948 wins International Prize for Sculpture at Venice Biennale
1986 dies in England

18
Salvador Dali

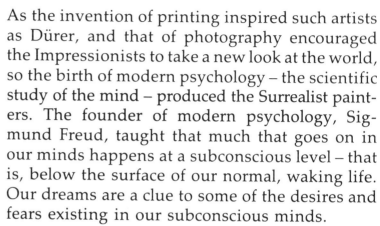

As the invention of printing inspired such artists as Dürer, and that of photography encouraged the Impressionists to take a new look at the world, so the birth of modern psychology – the scientific study of the mind – produced the Surrealist painters. The founder of modern psychology, Sigmund Freud, taught that much that goes on in our minds happens at a subconscious level – that is, below the surface of our normal, waking life. Our dreams are a clue to some of the desires and fears existing in our subconscious minds.

This idea of a vast dream-world inside everybody's mind excited a whole generation of artists. They called their work "Surrealism," meaning "Extra Realism." One of the leading figures of the movement has been the Spanish painter Salvador Dali. He painted scenes and objects with the clarity of the best photographs. At first glance, the

1904 born in Figueras, Spain
1925 first exhibition of his work in Barcelona
1929 settles in Paris, and is acclaimed leader of the new Surrealist movement
1940–55 lives and works in US
1980 retrospective exhibition held in Paris
1988 living in his home town of Figueras; now in retirement and no longer working

Right *Dali has been a great showman, as well as a great artist. Here, he is depicted standing in front of one of his own extraordinary paintings.*

representations in many of his paintings seems realistic or clear enough. But, a closer look suggests landscapes and scenery that seem both familiar and strange, just as they often appear in our dreams. An even closer look reveals even stranger things happening to ordinary objects. Clocks and watches, for example, bend over, as though made of dough. Other objects are not where you would expect them. Often in his works we see insects in odd corners of his paintings – perhaps expressing some deep fear in Dali's own mind.

Dali is a religious man. He has painted biblical scenes such as the Crucifixion. Artists had been doing this for hundreds of years, but Dali saw the scene from an entirely different angle. His *Crucifixion* looks down on the figure of Christ from above and behind. This was another aim of Surrealist art – to make people see familiar scenes and images in a completely new and startling way.

Autumn Cannibalism *is the title of this weird surrealist painting.*

19
Sidney Nolan

The outback – the vast stretches of desert or semi-desert that form a large part of Australia – has inspired many of the paintings of Sidney Nolan.

He was born in Melbourne, and, as a student, he copied the work of such established European masters as Picasso and the Surrealists. Soon, however, he was experimenting with new techniques, especially with the use of new paints and other materials, to give his pictures a bright, luminous look. He found in the hot, dry, red landscape of the Australian outback just what he needed to create a style all his own. Nolan was inspired, too, by events and characters in his country's recent, but colorful, past; above all, he was excited by the legendary outlaw, Ned Kelly, who fought a gun battle with police before being captured

1917 born in Melbourne, Australia
1938 visits Europe, first exhibition of his work by Contemporary Arts Society, London
1949 begins work on his famous series of "Ned Kelly" paintings
1958–60 visits and works in US
1988 living and working in Australia

Right *Nolan taking photographs of the empty, sun-scorched Australian outback from which he obtains inspiration for his work.*

and executed. Kelly's square metal helmet with its jagged eye-slit appears as a symbol in many of Nolan's paintings.

As his fame spread, Nolan traveled, recording in his highly distinctive style, the scenery and the wildlife of other lands, from Africa to Antarctica. He has given new meaning, too, to such biblical subjects as the *Temptation of St. Anthony* (the subject of some of Bosch's paintings, see page 6), and to the illustration of ancient Greek and Roman legends. One of his most exciting commissions has been to design the scenery for a stage production of Stravinsky's famous ballet, *The Rite of Spring*.

This individual, brilliant, and versatile artist is recognized as the leader of the modern Australian school of art which includes such original painters as Arthur Boyd and Fred Williams.

Nolan portrays an episode in Australian history: a sick member of the Burke and Wills expedition that set out to cross Australia in 1860.

20
Andy Warhol

The other artists in this book have painted scenes from the Bible, carved majestic statues, expressed their feelings and passions, or suggested half-hidden secrets of the mind. Andy Warhol has used such everyday objects as soup cans, detergent packages, or plastic bottles to give us a very different picture of our world.

He began his career as a gifted and successful fashion illustrator. Then, he became interested in methods of reproducing images, especially by a technique called silk-screen printing. He used it to present everyday objects in sequences of strong, bright images, varied by pattern and color. The results were so fresh and eye-catching that very soon his work had earned its own special name of "Pop Art." He also selected photographs of movie stars, and of news items such as

Left *The artist selecting prints in his New York studio.*

riots, wars, and traffic accidents, and presented them in the same way – as large, decorative posters.

Warhol's Pop Art has been just as much a revolution in our own time as the work of the Impressionists, Cubists, or Surrealists was in their day. It has shown us the qualities, good and bad, of today's industrial consumer society; and by, its originality, it has helped to change standards of design.

Warhol also made experimental films, with such titles as *Eat, Haircut*, and *Empire* – the latter was a filmed study of New York's Empire State Building, recording changes of light and activity around the famous skyscraper through one eight-hour period. These are all ways of keeping us alert to the world around us – the duty of the artist in every age and culture. Sadly, this revolutionary artist died in 1987, aged only fifty-six.

Above *Warhol's study of flowers uses silk-screen printing and acrylic paints.*

1931	born in Philadelphia
1950	graduates from Carnegie Institute of Technology, New York, and begins career as fashion illustrator
1962	leads a group of artists in the creation of Pop Art
1987	dies in New York

Glossary

Abstract art Painting or sculpture in which the artist uses colors and shapes, instead of a realistic portrayl of what is seen.

Bronze Alloy (mixture) of copper and tin. It is usually cast as a piece of sculpture by heating into a molten state and pouring it into a mold in the shape of the sculpture, then waiting for it to cool and harden.

Caricature Drawing or painting exaggerating the most prominent features of a person's appearance for comic effect.

Chiaroscuro Italian word meaning "light-dark," describing a style of painting with strong contrasts of light and shade.

Cubism Style of abstract or semi-abstract painting and sculpture, dating from about 1910, based on cubes and other geometrical shapes and patterns.

Engraving Method of printing by cutting lines into a metal plate, so that ink in the lines is transferred to paper. Etching is a form of engraving, using acid to eat, or etch, into the plate.

Fresco Italian word meaning "fresh," describing a method of painting on fresh, damp plaster on a wall or ceiling. As the plaster dries, the painting dries with it.

Impressionism A movement in painting developed in France in the 1870s, in which the artist used color and light to record an impression of a scene.

Perspective The way in which objects appear larger or smaller, depending upon their distance from the eye.

Porcelain Fine and delicate kind of pottery or earthenware.

Rococo Style of art and architecture, popular from about 1700 to 1750, noted for its delicacy and detail.

Silk-screen printing Method of printing, using a stencil (patterns cut out of a sheet of fabric) and a section of stretched silk cloth (or other material with a fine mesh) through which ink reaches the paper. It is used in the design and printing of fabrics, posters, signs, and labels.

Surrealism French word meaning "extra-real," describing the type of painting developed in the 1920s, inspired by dreams and ideas about the subconscious mind.

Woodcut A carved block of wood with areas or shapes forming an image that can be covered with ink and printed on a sheet of paper. One of the oldest forms of printing.

Further reading

Art Ventures: A Guide for Families to Ten Works of Art in the Carnegie Museum of Art (Carnegie Institute, 1987)

Enjoying the World of Art by Pierre Belves (Lion Books, 1966)

Great Painters by Piero Ventura (Putnam, 1984)

A History of Art: From Twenty-Five Thousand B.C. to the Present (Random House, 1984)

How Artists Work by Pierre Belves (Lion Books, 1968)

Investigating Art: A Practical Guide for Young People by Moy Keightley (Facts on File)

Pablo Picasso by Ernest Raboff (Doubleday, 1982)

True or False? Amazing Art Forgeries by Ann Waldron (Hastings House, 1983)

Woody Watches the Masters: Four Great Artists by Mary L. Jones (Vantage Press, 1985)

Index

Works of art are listed under
the artists' names

Abstract art 5, 36
Australian outback 42

Barcelona 40
Baroque art 15, 17, 37
Berlin 34, 35
Biblical scenes 11, 13, 16, 31,
    41, 43
Black artists 5, 30
Borgia, Cesare 9
Bosch, Hieronymous 6–7, 43
    Garden of Earthly Delights 7
    Seven Deadly Sins 7
    Parable of the Sower 7
Boyd, Arthur 43
Braque, Georges 36
British Empire 30

Cave painting 4
Caravaggio 17
Caricature 18
Ceramics 37
Chiaroscuro 5, 17
Chinese art 20
Collages 36
Commercial art 19
Corot, Jean Baptiste 26
Cubist art 5, 36, 45

Dali, Salvadore 40–41
    Crucifixion 41
    Autumn Cannibalism 41
Da Vinci *see* Leonardo
Degas, Edgar 21
Design, principles of 11, 45
Drawing 9, 10, 34
Dürer, Albrecht 10–11, 40
    Apocalypse 10
Dutch artists 16, 22

El Greco 4, 14–15
    Burial of Count Orgaz 15

St. Jerome 15
View of Toledo 15
Engineering 8
England 18, 19, 22, 38
Engraving 10, 19, 34, 35

Fascists 37
First Impressionist
    Exhibition 25, 27
First World War 34
Florence 9, 12, 13
Fragonard, Jean 26
France 9, 22, 24, 25, 26, 27, 28,
    29, 30, 31, 36, 37
Fresco painting 5
Freud, Sigmund 40

Gandhi 32, 33
Gauguin, Paul 28

Hitler 35
Hogarth, William 18–19, 34
    Election 18
    Gin Lane 19
    Horlots Progress 18
    Marriage a la Mode 18
    Rake's Progress 18
Hokusai, Kasushika 20–21
    Ukiyo-ye 21, 32
Holland 6, 16

Impressionist painters 5, 23,
    24–5, 26, 27, 28, 31, 40
Indian culture 32
Inquisition 14
Italy 8, 10, 15, 22

Japanese art 20–21
Jesuits 14

Kelly, Ned 42, 43
Kollwitz, Käthe 34–5
    Death series 34

Peasants' War series 34
Pieta 34
The Weavers series 34

Leonardo 4, 8–9, 11,12
    inventions 9
    Mona Lisa 9
    scientific drawings 8, 9
    The Last Supper 9
    The Virgin of the Rocks 9
Luther, Martin 11

Manet, Edouard 21, 27
Metal casting 5
Michelangelo 4, 12–13
    Creation of Adam 13
    David 12
    designs dome of St Peter's
        Basilica
    Last Judgment 13
    Pietà 13
Monet, Claude 24–5
    Impression – Sunrise 25
    Thames series 25
    Waterlilies 25
Moore, Henry 38–9
    Madonna and Child 34
    North Wind 39
Morisot, Berthe 5, 26–7
    In the Wheatfield 27
    Poplars on the Seine 27
    The Artist's Sister 27
    The Cradle 27

New York 44, 45
Nolan, Sydney 42–3
    Ned Kelly paintings 42
    Temptation of St. Anthony 43

Paris 25, 27, 28, 29, 30–31
Perspective 8
Photography 24
Picasso, Pablo 4, 36–7, 42

Blue period 36
Demoiselles d'Avignon 36
Guernica 36, 37
Pink period 36
Sleeping Girl 37
Pop art 5, 44, 45
Pope Julius II 12, 13
Prado Museum 7, 15
Primitive art 37
Printing 10, 11

Religious painting 4, 6, 15, 41
Rembrandt 4, 16–17
   Portrait of himself with
     Saskia 16
   Portrait of his son 17
   The Anatomy Lesson 16
   The Night Watch 16
   The Staal Meesters 16
   self-portraits 17
Renaissance 8, 11, 12, 14, 36
Renoir, Auguste 27
Rijksmuseum 16
Rococo art 26
Royal Academy 23

St. Peter's Basilica 13
Savonarola 12

Sculpture 4, 5, 8, 12, 13, 34,
   35, 37, 38, 39
self-portraits 10, 17, 29
Second World War 34, 35, 39
Silk-screen printing 5, 44, 45
Sistine Chapel 12
Slaves 30
Spain 14, 15, 36, 40
Spanish Civil War 36
Surrealist art 5, 40, 41, 42, 45

Tagore, Rabindranath 5,
   32–3
   Nobel Prize 33
Tanner, Henry Ossawa 5,
   30–31
   Daniel in the Lion's Den 31
   Moses and the Burning Bush 31
   Raising of Lazarus 31
Tate Gallery 23
Titian 14
Toledo 14, 15

Toulouse-Lautrec, Henri 21
Turner, Joseph M.W. 22–3,
   25
   Bathing Scene 23
   Fighting Temeraire 23
   Rain, Wind and Speed 23
USA 20, 30, 31, 33, 44, 45

Van Gogh, Vincent 4, 28–9
   Bedroom at Arles 29
   Sunflowers 29
   The Potato Eaters 28
Venice 10, 14, 15, 23
Verrocchio 8

Warhol, Andy 44–5
   experimental films 45
   illustrating 44
   silk-screen printing 44
Watercolors 5, 10, 22
Williams, Fred 43
Women artists 5, 27
Woodcuts 5, 10, 21, 34
World War I 34
World War II 34, 35, 39

Picture acknowledgements

The illustrations were supplied by Bridgeman Art Library 7, 9, 11, 15, 17, 21, 23, 26, 27, 29, 37, 41, 45. Mary Evans Picture Library 19; Topham Picture Library 13, 39, 42. *Poplars on the Epte* by Claude Monet, reproduced by courtesy of National Gallery of Scotland. *Germany's Children are starving!* by Käthe Kollwitz, reproduced by courtesy of National Gallery of Art, Washington. *Sleeping Girl* by Pablo Picasso © DACS 1987. *Autumn Cannibalism* by Salvador Dali © DEMART PRO ARTE BV 1988. *Flowers* 1966 by Andy Warhol, reproduced by courtesy of Saatchi Collection, London.